"The pleasure I feel every time I poems *is that each one is fresh anu jilled with new-found insights. I compare each one to a wandering sunbeam cavorting along the surface of a crystal bowl causing cascades of erupting glints, beams, twinkles and bits of rainbows."*
– Bess Marcus, co-author of *My Father*

"Barbara Novack is a writer of destiny who sparks the reader's essence. I treasure her work, its power, gentleness and care. She is a poet beyond the ordinary, a great writer."
– Dawn Martin, actress and artist

"Each of Barbara Novack's poems brings me to a place of emotional truth and clarity."
– Deborah Nagler, life artist

"Barbara Novack's poetry exudes warmth and humanity. I have never heard poetry with such humanity."
– Denis Gray, author of *Delia's Deed*

"Barbara Novack is an incredible poet with incredible insight into life's situation and emotion."
– Lorraine Conlin, poet and host of Poetry Tuesdays

"Barbara Novack's poems, filled with quiet, emotive language and varied and expansive images, express a crucial awareness of the world. She is a keen observer of people and the images come most passionately from her heart and her mind. As I read her poems, I connect with her response to nature, people, and intellectual ideas and she brings me in harmony with my own experiences. I love reading her poetry over and over again."
– Anne Dupré, author of *All About Isabella*

"Barbara Novack's poetry has a clean freshness not commonly seen these days."
– Maggie James, poet

"I have read Barbara Novack's poems and I had no idea I would enjoy poetry this much. I thank her."
– Paddy Noonan, entertainer and traveler

"Barbara Novack's gift is that she can capture an experience in a few lines of carefully shaped verse, and in the process communicate her sense of the moment's emotional quality. Poetry that can delight its readers should be encouraged, particularly in a world that sometimes seems to have lost its appreciation for the well-chosen word and the beauty of thought expressed through imagery."
– Dr. Kathleen Conway, author of *The Disclosure of Secrets* and *Negotiating the Sexual Contract*

"Barbara Novack's sensitive and observant eye, her alert and perceptive mind, her delicate and precise hand have recorded much worth sharing and much worth pondering."
– Dr. Robert Kinpoitner, Chairman, English Department, Molloy College

"Among Barbara Novack's many strengths as a writer are her eye for the telling detail, her ear for the cadence of natural speech informed by song, and her soul that always makes the human connection. She makes her people and the world they inhabit – the world we inhabit – come alive. Her poems remind readers of the value of words and the worth of the authentic voice."
– Patti Tana, author of eight collections of poems, most recently *Any Given Day*

Something Like Life

Something Like Life

Barbara Novack

JB Stillwater Publishing Company
Albuquerque, New Mexico

Library of Congress Cataloging-in-Publication Data

Novack, Barbara.
  Something like life / Barbara Novack.
    p. cm.
  ISBN 978-1-937240-09-7 (pbk.)
  I. Title.
  PS3614.09225S66 2012
  811'.6--dc23
                          2012032297

JB Stillwater Publishing Company
12901 Bryce Avenue, NE
Albuquerque, NM 87112
http://www.jbstillwater.com
20121119
Printed in the United States of America

To the Novacks, here and beyond,
for their love and support

and

To Dr. Mathew Lee,
healer, friend, inspiration

Acknowledgments

These poems first appeared in the same or similar form in the following publications:

Nassau Review
"Looking Glass," "Shadow Dancer," "Rejection," "Infinities," "In That Twilight Before Sleep," "Something," "Change," "Still Life," "Black Holes," "Definition," "Going Somewhere Else," "Thaw," "Billet Doux," "In the Nature of Connections: A Healing," "Chekhov, For Beginners," "September," "The Burning of the Shoes," "November," "Recipe," "A Rainbow in the Sand," "Eulogy" and "Brown Paper Bags"

The Cape Rock
"The Painters," "Elsewhere" and "Elegy"

CQ (California Quarterly)
"The Gulf: A War," "Father and Child" and "'The Frisbee Players'"

Slant: A Journal of Poetry
"Free Fall," "A Lesson in Quantum Mechanics," "In the Heart" and "Sound Effects"

Istanbul Literary Review
"A Matter of Weight," "Cross-Cultural Communication," "Boomerangs Come Back" and "Death Smells Like Old Shoes"

Avocet
"Ephemera"

Oberon
"The Explorers" and "Red Balloon"

Verve
"Theft"

Long Island Quarterly
"Cause and Effect" *and* "Too Far"

PPA Literary Review
"Naked Singularity"

Paumanok II, Interwoven
"Perpetual"

Creations Magazine
"Doesn't Get Any Better"

Xanadu
"Human Form with Light"

Long Island Expressions
"Sacrament (On the Southern State Parkway)"

Best of 2012
"The Woman in Black"

Author's Note

Something Like Life is thematically constructed. While, of course, you could dip into the collection at any point and read the poems individually, which is the way they were written, taken together, in each section, they form a narrative, and as a whole, they form a larger narrative. Whichever way you choose to approach the poems, I hope you enjoy them.

Barbara Novack

v

Table of Contents

Part One: Portrait

Part Two: Still Life

Part Three: Collage

Part Four: Landscape

Something Like Life

It is art that makes life.
~ Henry James

Part One: Portrait

*Every portrait that is painted with feeling
is a portrait of the artist, not of the sitter.*
~ Oscar Wilde

Free Fall

I wander the aisles
not admitting the purpose
eyeing the mirrors edging the ceiling
and the half globes of reflecting chrome
and the cameras mounted high
eyes
that I know
follow mine
watch my hands
read my mind.

I touch and fondle
the slithery deed
in book, pen, magazine,
candy bar and patterned hose,
nothing that I truly need
except
the need
to succeed,
a consummation that will be
like knowing all the answers
on *Jeopardy*.

I grab the prize.

And later
I will rationalize:
Sometimes you have to
free fall
to know you're alive.

A Matter of Weight

It grows, not solidity,
but a flaccid broadening,
a looseness, oozing
from the borders
over the sides, rolling
outward.
A center line, like a stick,
casts a mind-thin shadow
circling around
with the passing time
until its farther edge traces
a Buddha base
of abundance.
On such pillow softness we dream
restful ease and comfort, but
we worship The Gaunt One, The Sufferer.

Sin has a broad base, too.

The Woman in Black

She shimmers in the flat fluorescence,
a glossy magazine image
among the gnomes,
the drab-life drones:
blond sun-streaked hair
big black sunglasses
model-star-actress features
set in luminescent skin,
style
in a black sheath dress
and black high-heeled pumps.
This tall elegance
pushes a shopping cart
in the A&P
like me
except I
am in worn jeans
dirty sneakers
and floppy T-shirt.
She is who
I dream to be.
We all dream her,
the odd-sized and so carelessly dressed
women
and men
who turn at her passing
and sneak surreptitious glances.
She ponders the shelves
of the mundane
ignoring aisles filled
with the same
who ponder her.

Theft

His name was Philippe
and we met in the park.
He carried a sketch pad,
I my lunch in a brown paper bag.
His name was Philippe
and his accent was French
and his hair dark and his eyes soft.
My sandwich was American cheese.
He said he was an artist, recently arrived;
he asked if he could draw me.
I said, "I don't know why."
I did not think I was an interesting subject,
just a person eating her lunch
on a sunny spring day
in the park. But
I said, "Okay."
His pencil moved quickly
over the blankness,
his eyes following the movement.
It was strange, I thought,
that he did not look at me
when it was me
he was drawing.

There are people, more primitive than we,
who refuse to have their picture taken.
They believe it is theft

of the soul.

The drawing was
me
with a sensual beauty
I'd never seen
in a mirror.

I might have loved Philippe
if I'd ever seen him again.
He kept the drawing,
I kept the memory.
Is it theft to take
something
that only he
knew was there?

The Painters

The painters come
with their cans and brushes and rollers
to cover the lost colors
years have resolved to a wistful shadow
of what might have been.

I selected whites this time,
shades of purity,
searching for my truth
in the tenuousness
of untrammeled snow
in its moment in
the melting sun.

The painters come
and my artifacts huddle together
beneath splattered dropcloths
and I wonder who
did a room in midnight blue
and who in sharp citrus yellow
and who in peachy pink.
I wonder at the hope behind
the rainbow colors.

I huddle with the artifacts
in a dark void of silence,
lacking the passion of midnight blue,
citrus yellow, peachy pink.

They tell me, these painters,
it will be bold
when it is done.
I know

it is only
the blank page
to be won.

Red Balloon

You bought me a red balloon on the boardwalk
that sunny Sunday in May
when we met at the ice cream stand
and you had a white drip on your chin
and I a splotch on my nose.
We laughed,
and it was that warm laugh of sharing,
not the guffaw that
points out the awkwardness.
There is no awkwardness in sharing
as we found following the red balloon coasting along
        the sky
in the salt-scented air of May afternoon that turned to
        balmy evening;
we followed the red balloon.
It would be nice to say we let it go
and soared with it
in that moonlit night,
but
life is not that way.

Saying goodbye and well that was nice,
with an ending smile I let it fly.
But still he stood at the boardwalk rail.

Watching it longingly as it crossed the moon
I realized
love could just be
a red balloon.

Shadow Dancer

I never asked a question of night
that I could not answer
in other images
with tendril clouds across the moon
to darken my trespasses.

I leave footprints,
the earth too sodden
to hide me well:
I sink in it, to it,
the suction of me and it,
pulling
while I seek
a pure and icy moon.
And I do confuse my goal
and quest
with streetlamps
in the night,
hazy outline sketches
of glow
that attract me to the light.

I never questioned my footfalls
and I never stepped on cracks;
I never questioned direction,
only the way back.

And the doorway ladies,
shadow veiled, gowned
in aluminum foil,
glittered like the neon in
the sleek damp wet

of their toil.

The light of darkness turns lazy green
with a glimmer of sandwiched slivers,
and I trace the erosion of desert life
on parchment, they deliver.

I never asked a question of night
that somehow I could not answer.
But I never presumed to question day:
I remained a shadow dancer.

Looking Glass

A long time ago
someone
gave me a package of pink paper
for my printer.
I'd given him
glue
for pieces of his dream.
He was a swirling mass,
unformed.
He saw me
as his central star,
the one with the gravity
to pull him into being.
He did not know that I
was a black hole:
my magic was to bend time,
make it run slow,
make the past be now,
make it all one
until it imploded
into a tiny dense ball
of compacted fate.
My magic was to attract.
He saw me as the light
at the end of the long, dark corridor.
I was merely
a clear channel
to the darkness.

It is not all bad,
that sort of misunderstanding.
It passes the time

pleasantly enough.
After all, we do not wear masks
but mirrors.
And we leave
with the image
of ourselves.

A long time ago
someone
gave me a package of rose-colored paper,
a parting gift surprise.
I have kept it, a memento
of who I might have been
seen through the filter
of loving eyes.

And that, in the end,
was his magic,
my misunderstanding.

Dreams, Tinsel and Otherwise

He slid out of his skin
and lay beside me
no hide
all naked vulnerability.

It was the shimmery time
dark turns silver tinsel dream
to float between
now and now,
the place between two I-lands
in the stream where
stones wet with current
wash free

and, foam flecked, tumble together,
dissolving into one another,
silver sliver glitter surfaces
shining.

He slid
hand and thigh
upon mine
and trusted me
to be
as naked as he.

I was there
waiting, wanting
but I was only what I willed.
A silver tinsel dream
floated between.

Rejection

Leaves fall hard and shatter,
their colors preserved
like Tiffany glass.
You lie among them, stricken, shattered
broken on the season dream of spring.
"I thought you were the one," you cry.
"I thought you were the one."
I hoped you would be; my unspoken reply.
But I accept the not of it;
you whine.
Then you scramble to your feet, brushing shards away,
straighten to your height
and prevaricate, saving face.
"I never said what I said, never
thought what I thought, never
dreamed what I dreamed."
Or words very similar.
It is sad.
As if I don't remember you saying, "I love you."
You want to erase your error, and
I understand.

I didn't want to hurt you, but I had to.
There is no other way
to tell someone
the season is fall,
the future is barren and cold,
and the leaves are falling and shattering
like Tiffany glass.

Cross-Cultural Communication

We stand in the kitchen
drying the dinner dishes
placing them on their shelves,
quietly, civilized:
a few words mis-said
some points made with well-aimed arrows.
We are quiet, civilized
simmering.

The refrigerator hums.
The clock ticks.
The earth spins.
The plates clack against each other
as they are placed in neat piles.
The earth spins.
The clock ticks.
The refrigerator hums.

I sigh to let off steam.
His chest rises and falls
as air hisses
from his lips.
We sigh in unison.
It is not the soft satisfied sigh
we share as aftermath
tucked together like spoons
when our sighs coincide.
It is more like the sigh we share
stuck
in city traffic, horns
blaring, cabbies cutting in
and out.
The look in his eyes those times

– this time? –
holds a longing for a home not here,
a place sweeter and more serene.

"I stay go," he says,
pidgin English, Hawaii-style,
with a syntax all its own.
They teach the kids in school there
to speak the language properly
losing the lilt, the Pacific breeze
the palms' sway
to communicate in the monotone
of the broader world.
"I stay go," he says,
letting his words sing
their own tune.

"I stay go"
means I am going.
But I find comfort in
its strange oxymoron sense:
The constancy of going
is in stay
so, of course,
it means what it says
and doesn't.

Infinities

Sitting on the Fire Island dunes at night,
you and I
looked out at where sky and ocean met,
unable to discern
the meeting of infinities.
It was there, out there
in the starlit blackness,
at the end of the luminescent water,
beyond reach.

We had eaten dinner
at a nice restaurant
and had taken a walk afterwards
along the sand
down to the water.

Life lights faded behind us
and sounds were sand absorbed;
there was just the darkness
and us.

We sat shoulder to shoulder
on the sand,
shoes in hand,
and stared out at the unlit night.
It was strange, we remarked, to see nature pure,
without external light.
It was sad, we knew, to sit shoulder to shoulder
on the beach
with no internal heat.

We had discussed just that
over dinner

at the nice restaurant,
and it weighted our walk,
sinking our feet in the sand,
and it sat with us on the dune
as we stared into the night, realizing
we would never know
the meeting of infinities.

The Explorers

I stand in the shower
wash my hair
two three four times
run the soft cream soap suds
over hill and valley
surfaces
a lunar terrain
alien and apart
and devoid of life.
"One small step for man,"
the first explorer said.
"Magnificent desolation,"
the second added.
They traveled over her surfaces,
these explorers,
and never knew her at all.
Never knew if moisture
would tamp down the dust
seep to the center
and soften the soul.
Never knew if those
hills and valleys
could bear the weight
of more
than their boots.
That knowledge
was not
their intention.
She was just
one small step for man and
magnificent desolation

to explore.

I feel beaded droplets dripping
in the valley
where my heart beats.
If they had rested there
they might have returned
with more
than stones.

Phantom Pain

In the fetal brain,
a pattern forms
of the body as it should be,
arms, legs,
fingers, toes,
a road map
that remains
even if the road is never built,
if an arm or leg
never develops.
And that limb that never was
is felt.
It reaches up
to get a cup from the shelf.
It aches
and falls asleep
and pins-and-needles tingles
when it awakes.
It is there,
a living part of a person,
existing only
in the mind.

In the fetal brain,
a pattern formed
of my beloved.
A map of sorts
of shape
and sound
and essence.
I know him;
I feel his presence.
He is there,

a living part of me.
And a love that never was
is felt.

Ephemera

I was the wild tree
that grows in sidewalk cracks,
braving life that will not yield:
I would not yield.
I was golden yellow light,
summer,
an intensity tolerated because the days are long
and the nights are balmy
and the breeze is soft on naked skin.
Summer presses but does not push.
I was the storm that quick-darkens
and flashes light
and rolls its sound across the sky,
breaking solid blocks of heat
to pebble drops
on windowpanes.
I was calico,
a madness of color
that makes people smile.

I was youth,
merely a mood
that changed.

The tree was pulled up by the roots,
the street repaved.
Golden yellow light faded
to autumnal dusk.
The storm aged, white and silent
and cold.
And the calico was cut

to a pattern.

I remember the fireflies
I used to catch and bottle
to own their light,
to save a beauty
that gasped and died.

And only now
can I empathize.

In That Twilight Before Sleep

Things are only different
from what they are
in that twilight
before sleep
when possibilities rise
and reality drifts
away.
It is not sleep yet
where dreams attach meaning
to random brain impulses,
a fireworks display of neurons,
but sparks fly upward,
catching on the blue-gray haze
smoke smudging
the twilight sky.
It is not sleep yet, but
it is dreaming
and I hear words
and see images
and attach meanings
I prefer
to the sparks
that could never
be fire.

Something

Reaching for something
that was of me,
I watch the sun set low,
washing me in its embered glow,
a cleansing I would rather
have not be,
sadness to fill the space between
where I am and where
I might have been;
something was
a part of me,
sadness fills where it used to be,
and I must pause
to remember what it was.

And if I could remember now
how it felt, those feelings now
would return,
some thing that I learned.
And I watch the sun set low
and I am bathed in its glow
and I've paused for the show,
but I would rather
not know.

Memory is a fragile thing,
crystal lives that will not ping;
they are not pure.
Memory is just a game
of illusions that remain,
and I'm never sure.

I am angling for that sky,

lavendered with day gone by
leaning like a flower for the sun,
but it is done.
All that's left is me standing here
with feelings that are not as clear
as memory will soon make them be.
All that's left as I walk on
is the feeling that there's something
I should have done.

Change

Fallen, amid dried and faded leaves,
brittle, powdering to dust,
I drift on surfaces of cracked concrete
far from the road
of sure destination.
Silenced, weary, and wary of surprises,
I kick aside the red, yellow and brown
to make a path
where I step.
It covers quickly behind me, but
I walk in eternal present,
dulled,
watching each step,
so careful now
not to trip again
over life.

And watching each step,
I find pennies,
little copper pieces of insignificance.
A penny no longer buys anything,
is no longer worth the effort
to pick up when dropped.
So the pennies lie where they have fallen,
kindred spirits,
lost and unmissed.

I bend and retrieve,
bend and retrieve,
wiping away dirt and grime
until I see the shine
that made me smile

as a child.

Like words,
they add up
to meaning,
significance in the finding,
in the gathering and polishing,
in the sound they make
together.

Lost, then found,
they are change.

Part Two: Still Life

The aim of art is to represent not the outward appearance of things, but the inward significance.
~ Aristotle

Still Life

The bowl of fruit on the well set table
the pitcher unpoured
the cloth unstained.
What is the meaning
of the arrangement?
There is a longing
in the pieces,
still life.

Beneath the layers of dust
there is our life
half remembered.
Memento memories, artifacts
of an archaeological dig,
a hole in the ground,
sand to sift
for a bone or two,
a chip of clay hieroglyphed
and untranslated,
a lost language of being.

When they tell our story,
and they will tell it,
they will not get it right.
For we are motes caught in a stream of light,
moments trapped in amber,
pieces of an arrangement
no one can interpret,
yet still life.

A Lesson in Quantum Mechanics

All possibility
all possible states
cling together
in quantum superposition.
Traditionally, it is the act
of observation
that forces the particles
to choose
one state
or the other.

The aisle is long
the sides chosen
the particles to meet
at the end point
there to agree
to be
one state
not the other
under watchful eyes.

We have existed in
ambiguous states
a wave function where
all possible histories
all possible futures
all possible presents
have hovered together
and now
we are colliding with rock-solid
reality
a world that will

define us
forever.

All it takes, they say,
to collapse the wave
is a tiny disturbance
and the coherence of possibility
becomes unglued.

All it takes
is a tiny disturbance.

They say otherwise
we could possibly exist
as simultaneously
dead and alive
lingering
suspended.

The watchful eyes
could decide it,
but
all it really takes
is that tiny
disturbance.

I walk down the aisle
your eyes holding mine
your smile matching mine
till your hand is holding mine

and we choose
one state
over the other.

Cause and Effect

Today everything in the refrigerator froze.
The gallon of milk was a white ice block,
the soda cans bulged ready to pop,
pregnant with the moment.
It is April, spring, when life bursts open;
it is daylight savings time, when days stretch
like a rubber band
to hold all the growing things and expand,
pushing night into its dark corner
of dustballs and thoughts of the not-done.
And yet,
the food is frozen,
the nourishment unconsumable.
There is nothing in the waste of winter held,
refusing to yield.
The orange shattered when I dropped it.
The eggs were solid. I shook them to be sure.
I do not know if freezing spoils them.
But other eggs are frozen
later to be mixed
to yield, perhaps,
other pregnant moments.
I stare at the glaciated abundance
and wonder
if I have been reminded, this April,
of the cruelty.

The Gulf: A War

The words are grains of sand
folded into dunes
that shift with the wind
but do not change;
the meaning is
the vastness of it all,
the emptiness.
The words are small
and swirling,
clouding the sky.
Grains of sand change nothing;
only the dunes
survive.

Geometry

Out of fear, you and I make geometry.
Lines, barriers, fences
straight and sure
divide our life,
a fateful adjustment
to the world.
We create desirable abstract shapes
to hide within,
taking refuge
from impermanence and change.

Abstract lines defend against nature;
fixed flat planes transform
the changeable world:
three dimensions disturb.

We live amidst the unknown,
boxed into this stale stability,
denying loss and disorder
with rigid lines
that cannot bend.
But we both know life inevitably collides
with lines.
Life inevitably shatters
geometry.

In the Heart

We have become, in our baby boomer dotage,
experts on pain.
Twenty years ago we agreed
to have no regrets,
youth seduced by that impossible possibility.
Now we meet again,
you the certified specialist
in treatment
and I the writer
who has woven that decades-long thread
into a tapestry of words.
It is a reunion
of sorts and kinds,
and we come with significant others
who do not think to twist their rings
with uncertainty
at the sight of you and me.
And we hold up our drinks like shields,
then lower our defenses
and smile.
And we talk about who we are supposed to be
and what we are supposed to know
until we lapse into the silence
of who we really are
and what we really know.

You tell me all pain starts in the heart.
Actually you say the chest,
but you are a science person
and lack a certain verbal lyricism,
being technical and literal, but
the way you look at me when you say it

is eloquent.
You may be explaining how it radiates
through muscles and nerves
to the shoulders and neck
and around the ears
and to the cheek and chin
and lips,
but the way you look at me
warms all those places
with kisses.

Perhaps it is textbook true
that all pain starts in the chest,
but as we sit
constrained by the lives we've made,
I think we both know
it starts in the heart.

The Dark of Light

Flying above cotton wool clouds
looking as I'd expect
when they should look strange
when I am among them:

I know why clouds form,
why the sky is blue,
why planes fly.
Why then do I grip the armrests
as if the plane would fall and
my clenched fingers could hold it up?
Why then do I marvel at
the white fluff and think I could
step out and walk on it?
Why then does the blue
seem like a pool I could swim in
if I could but touch it?
I cannot hold clouds or sky in my hand;
they are not what they seem,
not white, not blue,
not substance.
I cannot hold the plane in the air,
hoist it with my grip on its meagerest part.
I am encased in this dream
of substance
when all is mere illusion.
And I turn from the window,
from the unshielded sunlight
of knowing,
to the darkest part of myself

sitting beside me.
He smiles,
looking as I'd expect
when he should look strange.

Definition

The falling down rising up
morning, sly-eyed,
creeps past the bottle,
lightly tipped,
and stains,
and scatterings,
and I rumble,
feeling vaguely
something
like a body
stuck to night
and glued
vaguely
to you.

And it is too bright,
this pale waste,
and too sharply
etched.
It defines too clearly
this hollow vagueness,
this nowhere room
of Holiday Inn greens and blues,
the restful hues
of easy lying.

Dying is
a bottle lightly tipped,
staining.

Going Somewhere Else

Nothing is someplace
somewhere,
a span of and,
elseness,
time all sanded
out,
the narrow neck coughed
clear
of here.

Oh, I know places.
Been to.
Gone through.
Passing towns' sighs
along a narrow two-lane
go-coming, standing still.
It's all lost, less the grave.
The markers gone.
Burma Shave.

We could say
Australia! –
the earth's end placeness of it,
an excuse for nowhere –
till it came next door
and we could exchange cups of sugar
and kangaroos
over late morning coffee
recipes.

The simple ease
of near

made going somewhere else
still here.
Too close,
still an almost,
still an edge
to navigate
too carefully,
the narrowness
of space's time
that walks a window ledge.

It slides away,
shifting dunes,
the last of the ruins
going somewhere else,
easing out
with a whisper merely.

Nothing is
someplace
where the glass sneers
clearly.

Black Holes

Theorist Suggests "Black Holes" May Be Explosive
~ New York Times

They say now
black holes explode
in the end state.
Subatomic particles pair
and disappear,
one falling in
to eternal nothingness
and its mate
flying off
into space
at a catastrophic rate.
They say now
black holes, as they die,
lose mass,
and radiate
the half-pairs
in apparent heat.

Quantum behavior,
they say,
is at last relative,
and even the darkest places
conform to laws
of thermodynamics.

The black hole
was supposed to be cold,
a pulling place
of no escape.
But now, it seems,

even darkness provides.
We deal with heat
and a collapsing world
too dense
to pull apart.
But now, they say,
all laws apply:
one will fall
and one will fly.

Boomerangs Come Back

In the emptiness of space
an astronaut threw a boomerang
out
expecting
a continuing journey into the void
into the vastness
neverending
lost in time and space.

Into our emptiness
your words thrown out
into the void
of neverending
lostness.

The boomerang came back.
No one knows why.

There is a point
where time and space
converge.

You stand at the door
hand on the knob
looking back.

The Problem Is

The problem is
I cannot make the sun rise.

Once, waiting in darkness
on the rim of the Grand Canyon,
the air chill with night
and anticipation,
I saw that tentative light
pearling the sky.
The horizon glowed the rock tips gold,
the sky streaked and gleamed,
the rocks shed their night cloak,
shimmering red-brown,
and then the sun rose,
announcing morning
with a fanfare for existence.
And I thought
the first day
must have been like this,
all glory
to lift nascent hearts
and set them beating
and sing the song
all birds would learn,
all glory for the creatures
who seem so small.

It is a good idea
to remember such things,
to keep them close and safe
where they will not tatter and fade.
Such things are comforting and encouraging
when night stretches too long,

when darkness weights the soul.
Such things
cushion the spikes
of night.

For a week now
I have been holding that image,
I on the rim
in darkness
waiting for light, for day, for glory, for hope.
But I see only the glimmer on the edge of being.

The problem is
less the sunrise
than the darkness.

Thaw

The glacier recedes,
leaving tides high
and dangerous
and striations on the land,
tracking.

We have not spoken to each other
these many weeks,
occupying accompanying space,
repelling like the same-charged polarity
we were.
Sparks no longer flew.
It was the cold time,
winter of the soul,
all soft sentiment turned hard
and breakable,
easy to shatter.
And we stood on that thin sheet of slippery surface,
each convinced of walking-on-water rectitude
while our weight fissured the glaze.
We stood our sinking ground
resolutely.

I do not know what changed our minds.
Perhaps it was not quite being able to remember
what started it
this time.
Perhaps it was just becoming too easy
to slither past the other.
Perhaps it was the mirrors
we'd turned to the wall.

This morning I made your coffee

and buttered your toast.
This morning your shower towel
wasn't on the bathroom floor.
This morning we saw our reflection
in each other.

Perhaps it was the fear
of what we were sliding into
that pulled us back.

And the glacier recedes,
leaving tides high
and dangerous
and striations on the land,
tracking.

Naked Singularity*

You lay on our white sheets,
freshly showered and smelling of soap,
and as you reached your arms out
for me
you said, "You are my dream."
And I wondered
if you were mine,
what I dreamed.
I traced the line of you
from between your eyes
down your nose
felt the indentation
above your lips
and where they meet
and the cleft below,
traced down
the line
between your halves,
what I have,
the flesh of you,
the warmth.
I rested my cheek
upon your chest
heard your heart beat
felt you so alive
and I could not remember
dreams.

* a point of matter so dense, with such powerful gravity,
that nothing can escape from it, not even light; a black hole

Billet Doux

When I got down to
the breakfast table
this morning,
I smelled the sweet soap
scent
of your shaving cream.
I sat in your chair,
drank from your cup.
You were gone,
as our night,
but you lingered,
a sweet surprise,
like a love note left
for me.

Father and Child

They sit together in the sunlight.
He holds the baby gently
in his arms,
intently studying
this being
he helped make.
It squirms against his bare chest;
he cradles it tenderly.
Strands of dark hair fall over his forehead
as he looks down
at the infant
so small
in his arms.

No madonna could be more serene
or worthy
of adoration.

In the Nature of Connections:
A Healing

On the hottest day of the summer
when we, heat blasted and melting,
our shapes as wavery
as the shimmered steamy air,
came together
to prick the bubble of pain,
I gave you poems
of wonder and awe
and gratitude for graces.

A fine cool whiteness,
a purity.

On the coldest day of winter
snow devoured, we
burst forth whole
as balminess and sunshine,
and I gave you poems
of blessings
in the unexpected.

A silken petal, a tender leaf,
a hope.

Your ancient art is renewal.
Mine is rebirth.
Together we recreate
the center,
the balance in the flow,
the tempering of heat and cold,
the glow.

Chekhov, For Beginners

Chekhov said
throw out the first three pages;
it takes that long
to get to the beginning.

And I may say
put aside the first three decades
sweep away their debris
cast off versions of the self
that should have molted
like early outgrown skins.
Much was misunderstood,
misinterpreted.
The guidebook for those places
has been reprinted,
the new edition totally revised.
History, after all,
is just memory compromised,
smoothed out,
its sags stretched to cover the chasms
of existence.

So put them away
in the safe place
where the fading photos stay
and know
it took all that
to get to
the beginning.

Part Three: Collage

*I want to reach that condensation of sensations
that constitutes a picture.*
~ Henri Matisse

Time and the Spinning Wheel

On the day of
the end of the year
my clock lost twenty minutes.
I hurried it along,
set it right,
but later,
if it was later,
the twenty minutes
were lost again
or still
or not still at all,
for time moved, the clock's hands
moved,
circling a space defined
by the wheel.
The twenty minutes
were caught in the gears
holding back
the end of the year.

The day spiraled onwards
nevertheless
lacking no necessary moment,
but my clock,
my life-time companion,
hesitated.

I was eager for the closing moments,
ready to pack the tattered year away,
ready to take out the new
from its wrapping paper,
shake it free, unwrinkled

in its bright whiteness.

My clock was old;
it kept its twenty minutes
to the end.
The smaller, sleeker, newer model
tells me now
what is
rather than
what later on
I would wish
to be.

Perpetual

He gives me a perpetual calendar
from his desk –
time,
days, months, years
in perpetuity –
as a memento, a memory
of him, he
who runs out
of time.
His river grows shallower;
it empties into a hole
he looks down daily
but tries not to acknowledge
though he mutters,
"I should not be doing this
(practicing medicine, he means)
this way."
He does that well
and
this thing, too,
this thing we all must do
ultimately,
this thing we wish
never were.

It is all time, anyway
his and mine, part shared
part traveled
alone;
the last part, he says
is always alone.
But I tell him,
"When I see you, it is

always good."
He smiles, shakes his head, says,
"This part
is never good."
"To see you . . .," I say.
He nods. "It just means I'm not there."
The packing boxes.
They're moving him
he doesn't know where.
They packed all his things
while he was gone.
He'd kept an office
at the university hospital,
professor emeritus, physician,
so many honors, walls papered with plaques.
Now they're moving him
out
to somewhere.
"I'm old news," he says.
"I gave them fifty years,
ground-breaking research,
built a lab, brought in
money,
and they close the lab
and move me out.
Old news."

He tries to be
philosophical.
The world is for those
with time.
The world is controlled
by the power he relinquished
and the bitterness
of those
who measure themselves
against his shadow

and find themselves
wanting.
The world is gobbled
by the hungry
and angry.
He sighs,
"Old news,"
too nice always
too tired now
to fight back.

So they came and
packed his things
while he was gone.
And he sits
amid the boxes that
will go somewhere
glad only that he's
not in one.

And he gives me
who loves him dearly
time
perpetually
to remember him by.

The Nature of Winter
for Mathew Lee

On this stark monochrome landscape
lunar in its
shades of gray
leafless branches filigree
against the slate sky
settled low over day-old snow.
I watch my breath
puff evidence of life, but
in this silent
end-of-times moment,
the world spins   ·
elsewhere.

The nature of winter is
a dear friend
dying.

Lovely!

September

The pear tree in the neighbor's backyard
drops its crop on the driveway
with hard thumps
like baseballs hitting a mitt.
But the pears roll, uncaught.

Once my father climbed to the top of the garage
where the pear tree branches stretch over the peak
and perched there, straddling it, plucking pears
and tossing them down to me. I
caught each neatly,
brown-green balls of sweetness, small and firm,
slapping into my cupped palms
and deposited in a large paper bag at my feet.
The pluck, the toss, the catch, the drop:
we had a good rhythm that sunny September
        afternoon.
And when the bag was finally full and the game ended,
my father lit his pipe, set it at a jaunty angle,
and sat secure and serene
up high against the bluest sky.

The pear tree in the neighbor's backyard
drops its crop on the driveway
with hard thumps:
the pears roll, uncaught.

I stand at the kitchen window
and stare out at the branches
so high against
the emptiest sky.

Death Smells Like Old Shoes

Death smells like old shoes
of lived-in comfort gone
stale and musty,
the warmth of wear
gone stiff and cold.

Death holds
the shape of life
hollowly.

Elsewhere

A snippet of found film
only minutes long
fifty feet of the past
scattershot and skittish
spinning a long gone world
bouncing from bungalow to bungalow
treetop to treetop
sky to road to sky
until it settles
like a skipping stone
on a swimming pool
and splashing bathers
forty years ago:

Then the world was young.
The future is an elsewhere there.
I was two, in my father's arms,
he teaching me to swim
holding me
safe
as I splashed in the water
I giggling, he laughing
joy in his little girl.
He hands me to my mother,
the ever unswimmer happy in an inner tube,
and she props me against her
my legs out on the tube
and I am hugged, safe
and smiling.
I stretch one leg high
enjoying
where I am

who I am.

I do not remember
a world so young;
we were then
older than
we'd ever been.

All that
is elsewhere now
lost
but for these moments.
I watch
over and over
knowing what will come
not knowing what will be
wishing I could once again touch
what we were.

The Photograph

A photograph of my father
found among those of
beach excursions in black and white
and him grinning boyishly.
He is young
in his twenties
sitting somewhere outdoors
his arm, obscuring his face,
outstretched and pointing
beyond the containing frame.

He is not my father yet
in the strangely compelling
face-obscured photo
and yet
he is
the always-father
of me.

My mother is putting together albums finally
of all the boxed photos weighing down the closet shelf,
the chaos of images organized
into orderly years
of scenery and smiles.

This small photo she tosses
on the discard pile
as a match for the blurred, indistinct and unknowable.
I grab it up.
"Why?" she wonders.
"You can't see his face.
It's no good."

I grab it up
this small photo
she cannot understand
in her quest to define
the past.

My father is gone
and I have been stuck since his death
in a repeating moment
burdened and leaderless.
And now, I
need not see his face to understand
the message in the arm
outstretched and pointing
defining a future
beyond the containing frame.

Stroke

I recognize her in there
in that unfamiliar
lightning struck being,
so small she seems.
She can't smile probably,
but I see a twitch, I think
behind the clouded plastic of the oxygen mask.
She grips my hand
squeezes twice for yes
again and again.

I recognize her in there
and find slivers of self
in the unclenched hand,
the fist of yesterday splayed,
in the twitches of muscles
the therapist said he felt in the still thigh
when she was asked to lift the log of leg.

I recognize her in there
stunned still
by half
struck silent
but for the squeezing hand
and eyes that know what I say
I'm sure.

I recognize her in there.

The Burning of the Shoes

It is an ancient tradition
and ritual,
and I'm not sure what
it's supposed to mean
and probably prayers should be
said,
but I don't know them.

She was a fastidious person,
and her shoes are all neat
and polished
and carefully nestled
in boxes
and plastic bags –
clean whites,
snappy blacks,
shining blues,
and a giddy summer strawberry red –
and, one by one, we
remove them from the boxes
and plastic bags, remove them
carefully
and drop them, one by one,
into a metal garbage can;
and when they are all there
in a disorderly tumble
she never would have tolerated,
we pour kerosene over them.
Then we light kitchen matches,
firm, strong, straight,
as she was,
and toss the flames in

to flame.
Orange, deep orange,
rises
like demons freed.
But what demons to dance here
where none were
before?
In one's last licks
comes
a flash of fire.

It remains
contained,
and merely burns
until it is all
only brown-black smoke
and ashes.

It is an ancient tradition
and ritual,
and I'm not sure what
it's supposed to mean,
but the shoes of the dead
are always burned.
And perhaps that is the prayer
of mourning:
the knowledge that
no one alive
could fill them.

Elegy

Scattered among the family, like leaves fallen
from the tree,
images in black and white
declare: I am.
Unlike the recent color photos
fading to nonexistence
like a dream,
these remain.
They are reality,
sharp and clear.
But who are these people
so staunch and proud,
dressed in their finest clothes
and posed so stiffly for their permanence?
And who are the others
at their ease?
They smile for the camera
that knew them
on front porches and stoops,
in living rooms and kitchens,
places that were home
somewhere.
There are no names or dates or places
written on the backs
of these family photographs.
These people trusted memory
for their immortality.
And now no one can remember
who they were.

November

The damp smell of earth at night
and woods so close,
pine and crisp country air,
and the gravel crunches beneath our feet
as we walk to the house,
white shingle with green trim,
from the matching garage
across the path that leads
down the hill and around the house,
down past the well house fortress
defended so many times
from attacking snowballers,
down to the garden
where mown grass was piled high
and we dove into its sweetness
and into the orchard
where we climbed the trees
and picked the apples
that made the jellies, jams and pies.

The lightbulb on the porch
in its white ceramic fixture
casts a warm and golden glow
on this frosty November night,
welcoming the children in
from the cold.

Part Four: Landscape

Any landscape is a condition of the spirit.
~ Henri Frederic Amiel

Brown Paper Bags

Tearing a brown paper bag
smooth, thick, dense
I hear a rattle as it bends in my grip
and a dull sound as it shreds,
releasing a memory redolent of
forest-fresh wood pulp
and September crayons
and bleach-clean new notebooks.

In the evening
bathed in golden incandescent light
the brown paper bags from the grocery store
were measured on the kitchen table against the open
    texts
and carefully cut
and smoothly folded down on the long inside
and over the cover edges,
a pocket miraculously appearing
into which the text neatly slipped

until all the schoolbooks sat
in their matching brown covers
with their subjects neatly lettered on the front:
arithmetic, spelling,
social studies, English–
an orderly world
of smooth sameness
carefully divided.

Now the supermarket bags are plastic
and grocery stores are extinct
and the children's books have stretchy covers
with Pokémon or Spider-Man,

or all things sports or Disney,
store bought, prefab and flexible reflections
of their time.

As perhaps ours were, too.

It was the '50s, after all,
that orderly world
Eisenhower and brown paper bags . . .
and Elvis on the horizon
to change it all.

"The Frisbee Players"

*The sculptures are full-size
representations of scenes from
modern life.... The beauty of
these figures is that, from afar,
they appear to be real people.
It is only up close that their
true nature can be detected.*

On the tree-lined lawn
amid the moving bodies
two of metal
frozen
almost toss a Frisbee
almost catch it.
Bronze-brown
in white shirts,
they are designed to catch life,
freeze a moment
for wonder.
So real, almost,
so like life, almost.
So very still.
Impassive faces
with dead bronze eyes.

The moving bodies pause
hesitate
circle warily
almost caught in the betweenness
of stopped time.

Something there

that does not like
the sunny-day, pulse-pounding,
face-flushed giddiness
that surrounds.
Something there
better seen in granite
in the still and silent place.
Something there
of shivers.
On the tree-lined lawn
two figures stand
frozen
in the almost moment
ready to toss
ready to catch
never to.

And moving bodies
circle warily,
unamused.

Sound Effects

From outside my window, I hear
feet running and
the voices of my neighbor Paul, my neighbor Bernard:
"Catch him! Trap him!"
"God, he's fast."
"Smoke, that's it, girl. Get him."
"Shit! He scared her off. Damn!"
"Gutless cat."
"But look at the size of him. Is he
foaming at the mouth? Do you think
he's got rabies?"
The feet scramble, thumping
on the grass and driveway, rustling
through the bushes,
the voices curse and grunt, grunt and curse,
and then
silence
and then
pop, pop.
I know the sound.
I used to think it was firecrackers
but no more;
too often now in the night have I heard the sound
distant
but not distant enough
and now
it is next door, in daylight, right outside
my window.
I wait, then emerge
from hiding.
The rat, huge and dead,
is on a shovel propped against the neighbor's stoop,

displayed like a trophy in the Wild West.
I ask Paul, I ask Bernard:
who shot him? whose gun?
They smile sheepishly,
they shrug.
I do not see the gun, but I know now
it is next door.

My neighborhood on the fringe of the city
was once quiet, and I felt safe.
Now there are rats. And guns.
And I wonder how long
both
have been there.

A Clean, Well-Lighted Place

It is the light of course but it is necessary
that the place be clean and pleasant.
~ Ernest Hemingway

They seek
a clean, well-lighted place
for comfort
and confirmation
and communion,
for the simplicity
of knowing
what is provided.
Essentials and frills
fluorescently lit
into an evenness of expectation
with soft music playing
in the background
smoothing voices to a murmur
of oneness.
It is all here
as if sanctified,
all wants and needs
fulfilled,
all doubts relieved,
the lost self
found
as they gather and gaze
and purchase indulgences.

Their years all behind,
they push their carts
along the aisles

in the supermarket.
Their years all ahead,
they check out
this week's fashion
at the mall.
They fill the empty days,
each reaching for salvation
in a clean, well-lighted place.

October Sky

Miles from ocean
a gull flies, sparkling white
against the clear blue
October sky.

I sit taking in
the last of summer,
watching the sun shimmer
orange tipped trees,
watching squirrels scurry
ruffling the leaves,
hearing birds chirp, sing and call.
It is a still Sunday
brown leaves rustle
across pavement in
a soft blade-sheathed breeze.
It is the last
of summer.
There is early barrenness
the warmth belies.
There is early sadness
the joy belies.

The gull knows,
miles from ocean,
far from home,
as it flies,
belying the clarity
of the October sky.

The Wave

The wave washes across the floor
where the newly wedded couple
dances and smiles.

Arrayed around the reception hall
family,
my mother, my uncle
the only two of the generation so numerous
when I was young.
We are the numerous now
and our generation's children
and the new generation just begun.

(And do these little ones,
so smooth, soft, powder-fresh and new,
see the grandparents and grand-uncles
        and grand-aunts – us –
as we did?
Are we now the huge alien skin-crumpled creatures
always reaching for them
whose strong smells smother
who clutch them to stiff chests
and slobber smiling kisses?)

The wave moves
across this floor.
The children's children
getting married, making homes, having children:
it's their time now.
Even we – boomers all –
are the past,
and our parents
too often only memories now

beloved to us
distant to them
non-existent to the next.

And the wave washes across the floor
where the newly wedded couple
dances and smiles,
inundating our time
leaving
in its wake
only theirs.

Life Lesson

On the grayest day of summer
he told me he'd decided
to stop treatment,
to do
nothing.

He'd stood again upon the brink
of the yawning chasm,
its jaws ready to clench,
its sharp teeth to gnaw, chew and wrench
the spirit from the bone
and then spit him up
to the other side,
and this time, he could not see
the other side
from where he stood,
just the jaws and black depths
between.

And this time he decided
to sit down upon the brink
and watch the breeze lightly fluff tree leaves
and watch the sun rise
and watch the sun set
and smell the grass and hint of ocean
and know the flowers
and their company of butterflies and bees
and listen to the birds
and see their colors as they fly
into the sun
that rises
that sets
and rises again

as he sits.

On the grayest day of summer
he told me
he'd decided
and was comfortable
with it.

He'd once called it
a Las Vegas game,
which side of the odds
you fall on.

In my eyes
he wins

knowing
doing nothing is
doing everything.

Eulogy

"Say something nice about him,"
they ask.
"But I really didn't know him."
I reply.
They grip my hands, tug at my sleeve
in sadness and in need.
"You lived next door to him," they say.
"You watched him clip his hedges
and tend his roses,
you shoveled his walk
when it snowed.
"Surely," they say,
"you have some words.
He was your neighbor."

I have paid my proper respect
to the dead,
said my proper condolences
to the living;
somber-faced and soft-voiced,
I have followed proper etiquette,
hoping no one will suspect
I did not know this man
whose walk I shoveled because he was old
and I was already doing my own,
whose hedges were neat
and roses red,
to whom I said a cheery hello in passing
because it never cost anything
and seemed a proper courtesy
to a neighbor
who smiled in return.
I did not know him

or particularly care:
I had my own concerns.

Yet it is I who am selected
to raise the moment, to toast the life,
a life as mysterious to me
as life itself.
"Say something nice."

It is a strange string
this thing we know
day to day
and think the least about.
The most precious beads
are the least costly.
Hellos and smiles.
A shoveled walk.
A perfect rose handed to me
over the backyard fence.

I cannot plumb his mystery,
but finding something nice to say
is easy.

Recipe

My grandmother's house
always smelled of baking.
Her stubby fingers and
strong arms
pounded dough
till it yielded
then gently
shaped it, sweetened it.

My grandmother did not know art.
Or music. Or literature.
She could not read or write.
And she baked
by touch and feel
and instinct:
she knew
when it was right.

My mother and my aunts, one afternoon,
tried to capture her magic,
contain it, commit it
to paper and perpetuity.
Each pinch of flour, salt, sugar
was greeted by a measuring cup
shoved gracelessly under her hand
and diligently recorded.
Ten of flour, four of salt, eight of sugar –
tiny amounts, multiple minuscule pinches
of this and that
they toted up, tallying repeatable measures
as my grandmother smiled and hummed
and ignored them,
baking on,

her calm, sure, strong hands
pinching, poking, flavoring,
shaping a world
of round challahs, crescent cookies,
rolled horn ruggelach and triangular hamantaschen.
I watched and laughed
and thought their effort
feeble and funny.
My grandmother would bake
as she always had
with no recipe.
And we would smell
the warm sweet smells
and eat the warm sweet delicacies.

My grandmother is gone.

We buy our cookies and we buy our challahs
cold and scentless, wrapped and sealed
from a supermarket.

But every once in a while
my mother
takes out a tattered piece of paper
and follows the measures so carefully recorded
that long ago afternoon.
And once again
there are crescent cookies
and triangular hamantaschen,
and the kitchen is filled
with warm sweet memory.

I sense her essence now,
my youth turned to age,
and wonder why I thought
there was so much she didn't know.
She came with nothing

but a feel
for sweetness
and left us
with a recipe
for life.

Sacrament
(On the Southern State Parkway)

On the tightly curving parkway, I
dizzy with speed
tense with route newness
exits and merges,
suddenly see a swirl
of giddy rose petals
floating from a car up ahead.
They dapple the roadway,
christen my car
and fill me
with blessèd mystery.

Human Form with Light

We are
skin shell and bone
structured to articulate
and retain shape,
holding all the parts
in place;
this dwells in darkness
I cannot know.
And we are
sparks flying upward
synapses firing
electrons jumping,
and Edison creates incandescence
and Einstein's e
flies light speed relatives
and we are
lanterns and lighthouses
and could be Christmas trees
if we but
allowed the joy.

A Rainbow in the Sand

By the curbside, sand ground fine
stone diminished to its merest particles
gray brown
almost colorless in the city.
And yet, as I step to cross the street,
I see a shimmering rainbow arc
beneath my feet.
I touch it tentatively with my toe.
The sand shimmers and shifts
but holds its magic.

I have been preoccupied this morning
with the day's troubles
with the mundane
that has ground me fine
like city sand, colorless,
to be trod upon,
and I have trudged,
head down beneath the too-bright light,
lost in dreary thought.
But I have touched my toe, this morning,
in a rainbow.
A reminder, so gentle, so tactfully discreet,
that beauty
and blessings
and even magic
lie at my feet.

Too Far

In Hawaii
they give directions
strangely.
Wherever you want to go,
you are told the street
beyond.
They say, "If you are at King Street,
turn around.
You've gone too far."
The turning around,
retracing your steps,
is part of the game of
going somewhere,
sort of circling your
destination
before landing.
Is it, I wonder, the island sense
of you can't really go
too, too far,
so why worry about it
or
is it the wry humor
of those who know versus
those who don't
or
is it just the shrug
of Paradise living:
who cares anyway
since it's all beautiful
and time, well,
it's different here,

isn't it?

Oh, some bring their hurry-up with them,
but even they,
when they see the soaring surfer's waves,
the soul-bursting sunsets,
the star-spattered night,
when they hear the symphony of swaying palms –
piccolo to oboe to bassoon –
even they sigh and smile
and slow their stride.

And I wonder,
is there such a thing as
too far?
Until you turn around,
too far is where you go.
Too far may be the destination
you didn't know you wanted –
and then
it is not
too far
at all.

Doesn't Get Any Better

eating blueberries
listening to the Beatles
reading the funnies
on a summer Monday
when I don't have to be anywhere . . .

eating oatmeal cookies
listening to Vivaldi
watching the rain
on a summer Monday
when I don't have to be anywhere . . .

sipping iced tea
listening to the cubes clink
putting my feet up
on a summer Monday
when I don't have to be anywhere . . .

but here

Index

About Barbara Novack

Barbara Novack, Writer-in-Residence at Molloy College, is also a member of their English Department. She founded and hosts Poetry Events and Author Afternoons, two reading series at Molloy College that bring contemporary poets and writers to a wider audience, and she presents programs and conducts workshops on poetry, fiction, and memoir in the New York metropolitan area. An award-winning writer, she is listed in the *Directory of American Poets and Fiction Writers* and in *Who's Who* and *Who's Who of American Women*. Her website is www.barbaranovack.com.

Also By JB Stillwater

Orphan Thorns
Lynn Strongin
ISBN: 978-1-937240-06-6

In this touching and often heart wrenching book, Lynn Strongin explores the beauty of the human soul and its ability to rise above physical as well as psychological illness.

Dark Salt
Lynn Strongin
ISBN: 978-0-9845681-4-7

In this collection of late works by Lynn Strongin, we find that perfect balance of salt and water spiced with symbolism and metaphor that poet Strongin does so well. Jewish Temple offerings included salt and Jewish people still dip their bread in salt on the Sabbath as a remembrance of those sacrifices.

A Thousand Doors
Matt Pasca
ISBN: 978-0-9845681-6-1

Pasca's work pays homage to Kisa Gotami's quest to save her son by finding a home where, impossibly, no suffering has befallen the inhabitants. In the end, A Thousand Doors testifies to the necessity of sharing our stories with courage and vulnerability, and how doing so can lead us further down the path of joy.

Notes

29698567R00080

Made in the USA
Lexington, KY
04 February 2014